Annulments

The Colorado Prize for Poetry

Annulments

Zach Savich

The Center for Literary Publishing
Colorado State University

For information about permission to reproduce
selections from this book, write to
Permissions, Center for Literary Publishing,
9105 Campus Delivery, Department of English,
Colorado State University,
Fort Collins, Colorado 80523-9105.

Printed in the United States of America.

Library of Congress Cataloging-in-Publication Data

Savich, Zach.
Annulments / Zach Savich.
p. cm. -- (The Colorado prize for poetry)
ISBN 978-1-885635-15-0 (pbk. : alk. paper)
I. Title. II. Series.

PS3619.A858A83 2010
811.6--dc22

2010020558

The paper used in this book meets the minimum requirements of the
American National Standard for Information Sciences-Permanence of
Paper for Printed Library Materials, ANSI Z39.48-1984.

1 2 3 4 5   14 13 12 11 10

The leper who has lost his nose and prays in his dark cave for a new one is common. The leper who has lost a nose and immediately cuts one off a dog and threads it to his face is the robust muse of the late William Shakespeare.

—Norman Dubie

To say many things is equal to having a home.

—Ezra Pound

Contents

Annulments

Poem After Last Night (1)

for David Bartone

A ladder built into the exterior of a truck,
all anything does is confide, every morning

beginning now, decency its own kind
of constitution, each step onto a balcony or

from a café with little outdoor seating,
not counting the city. "What year

is that from," the mother says. "First century
AD," says her son. "But that's a hundred

years."

Poem After Last Night (2)

for Jeff Downey

We proceed by pattern and anomaly, had
no money but lived above a bakery

and a florist, just-aged flowers free
in a trough. I liked how you called the street

I always take "the secret way," two fingers
held to a passing dog.

Poem After Last Night (3)

for Hilary Plum

We go to the cinema merely
for the light, view of alleys

from a balcony, to be in
the world and it is mythic:

zinnia market in the churchyard,
onions in mesh, daylit moon

a watermark on foreign currency.

The Mountains Overhead

1.

I sang: *Tell me of the heart which exists*
in which to continue is not
to confine

2.

Then dreamed I sang so loudly, I woke
myself singing

The cygnets' feet were lost in snow

The cygnets were lovely because footless

3.

Our augurs read their veils

What's sensible isn't seizeable, you said, waking

4.

Size-up-able

So I received lovingly all four-in-the-morning birdsong I was
a cutting-board for

Be how you were, be how you were

5.

You may only sing to dedicate a song

6.

You may hang your dresses on the back-
yard's line and you may rest here

You may work in a mine where you see yourself in
the rock and every day remove a piece
as large as your body

7.

I could never hide the mountain

Our talk over music
over wind

8.

To bring you to this:

We row out now over the lake where stars are
these muscles sobbing makes

Slashed across nightsky like bones
in owl droppings

9.

Star exhaust

Have fun, we said for goodbye

10.

These seconds whole months
were once

11.

Literally: to found meaning
to founder

Every pause, a cause

Every bow, a vow

At each footfall, landfall

12.

So I pressed my fists against my eyes then drew
hot air balloons to the cabin walls

You sang: *We touched in each other countries*
we will separate to

I sang: *As with water moving below*
I was building a house on your frozen

13.

Then dreamed land had a finger in
one ear, the wind

14.

I actually mailed rose petals once

Added extra stamps, as if it mattered

Sent them the quickest route, as if

15.

Aren't you wondering what my thigh feels like?

16.

I sang: *You would love it here, because I'm here*

You sang: *My cheek is softer where it touched your neck*

I sang: *I will hold you like it is enough*
for a singer to hold a single word

You sang: *Don't you always hold the door an extra second,*
hoping?

17.

Found holding anyone is actually not like holding a strip of moonlight

Found the hair on my tongue was actually my tongue

18.

I walked home—you can see it in my eyes

19.

When you pass

When you passed your hand over the rose,
I turned

Imagining one of those cameras that extends
a whole leaf if shown a torn half

Never mind if half has grown since its tearing or
if everywhere you look, tears

20.

Are you looking?

Look, we used to say

We only say: used to say

21.

Look, the bridge runs directly along and over
the river, never touching banks

22.

And if you shake your head in line
with windmills or any seasonally closing gate,
wouldn't it be like two trains leaving beside themselves, appearing
still?

No *no*

23.

When the lake froze, I crossed it

To a shore closest in the coldest

24.

Can't say to land: think of me

Or: you held me in place, in places

25.

Sang: *I needed you because how many times did*
I watch you dress?

26.

Whole months we kneaded as much
flour as the dough would hold into the dough, thinking
when it stops holding you
may punch it down, or the snow
may also stop

27.

My tattoo, a human coverall

28.

Ground rules:

That which can't be found being standard

What we really wanted was the best

Our needs precede us

The edge of doom is doom

29.

And so in the sixth month of winter twenty-two
years old I flew west

Artichoke of dawn
Hanging-grey apron dawn
Housewife dawn
Newsprint dawn hitting a stoop

Always behind me as I went

30.

Singing: *And here you are coming toward me*

Everything nearing, blooms

Water cold enough to cut

I could go on

31.

As though the end of harvest were not
farthest from harvest

As though reunion were not so close to ruin

32.

Singing: *This loss holds every loss*

Heigh-ho! Heigh-ho!

33.

Even the bottom of the sea is made of land,
thus cruel

Dante: *Here the earth produces of itself*

34.

Once, you said we built the rides because
we were already screaming

Built the mines because we were
already digging

35.

As every time speaking of dawn, I mean, meant
the fires which process the coal, fired
by coal

36.

Dawn in the clouds like gold in a tooth

37.

And you said, waking: *If this is a desert, I
will wipe sand from your skin*

38.

I'd often wake to you pacing a cramp from your foot

On the rug like the song in a shell

39.

While across the river, a student
asked the man with his telescope what's
so special about the moon tonight

Palatable moon

40.

Then a man we saw at the dance club dressed all
in white and carrying an orange

41.

As light is the light around a light

42.

I could see by your look

43.

I wanted a gentle way of waking you, so I let

So I let a tissue
sift to your face

Features rose like roots under a road

As crows fall from wires so the wires won't fall

As swallows lift on behalf of the porchwall

The crows: hearing our voices through wires

44.

We measured heights against the kitchen jamb, as though
the floor wasn't shifting

45.

Dawn stripping you like a cat
clawing a band of wallpaper

46.

Be how you were, be how you were

I mean more

47.

I sang: *Afraid I might say your name when asked*
my own

And: *I have waited a long time to say please*

48.

Whatever it means when berries outlast leaves

Or the fact of each match being lit from the last

49.

Each match as its own
first fuel

50.

Or needing to break one's mast on the bridge or
go back to the burning dock

The mast changed to a gnarled desert tree

Sail lifted to a gull

51.

The horses hold themselves like torches so they
won't burn like themselves

52.

So I wrapped myself in you as into a movie screen

Sang: I will be happy again, but not as happy

53.

Afternoons, we watched the benign gags
of silent films

Though not *as* films

If you ordered a rose, you'd get
a thousand on your porch

I wanted to draw you like the lungs or a lightning rod
or a bath

54.

I drew your picture by holding
my brush over a shaking tray

55.

The blind man in the market grabbed you, sang:
Tell me with your hand how the earthquake felt

In the public library,
you washed your hand

56.

He said he could still see red

So at dusk one day of invasion parachutists appeared
to divide and bloom against
a rusting sky

As though any shadow might divide and bloom

He watched the girls on the shore gather
red berries in the parachutes
of their skirts

Seeing only the fruit

57.

Remember where you were when?

Where you are?

Or one who had been hiking or asleep and so hadn't
yet heard?

58.

If the road is shaped like an S,

you know there were mountains

59.

My road-worn spine

There's a reason they keep repeating the chorus

And only sing the names of songs

60.

I have stayed two months on my way to you

At night we wash our hands with
our hands

We call it praying

61.

And there is a tribe that carries water for months

in their cheeks, their cheeks
hanging to their bellies and they never swallow

62.

Birds migrating in circle formation, turning like
a wheel,
they each have only a wing

Flying like bottles cast from an island, love

63.

Recall: I bent my brow
to the back's small

64.

I, candle sun melts

I, your second spine

65.

Is there any pilot light that's large enough?

Yuccas grow on the excess, the only hills: of slag

Piñon pine, thistle, oaten grove

I sang a private song

66.

I slip out now across this braided
loaf of land, a pretty stretch

Sun a dial tone

67.

Wanting to be continuous yet distinguished

Never building, but sprouting

This full-body callus

I bathe in a river

The light doesn't wash here, it lathes

A Young Man's Song

68.

For a beard I wear a smear
of oil I found in a ditch

Without the man, the beard is only odor

I sang: *We have only ever sat trying not to touch*

69.

Walking, so aware we were touching

Thistle

Granite scape

To leave being to meet

70.

Does dawn as of purple glass of very early
thickening look darker because we're awake in it?

I don't stop to wait for you, I hurry after

71.

The creek bed frosted like it isn't dry

The pump in the lawn, a lean dancer

Glove in the road,
sunning lizard

Day diving at me like the winking of a smoke detector's light

Once a minute

I remember love

72.

So many things are there until I look

73.

Inoperable only means unsuitable for opera

74.

Now a brood follows, so alone, dilating me, exfoliating dawn

As sulfur out a smokestack so tall we don't
believe

75.

Sang: *Tell me a secret I don't know I have*

76.

So I spend a week here, have been carrying
a Thing so precious any touch dissolves it, but to prove
its worth, meaning, destroy it, now, I need
to go on, so I
hold it against you

77.

Observed rightly after: two waxwings in chase lifted
seed from a grain cache, dropped it as
they lifted onto
a field as though in a shadow or map of
their chase, imagine it growing, lying in it, brushing
your hand over the grass and
the seed springs . . .

78.

We may rest here

79.

What I want is still harder

A possible letter at a slant in the box

80.

The wind appears to re-leave

the stripped limbs
by moving them

81.

Definitive, to keel: to stir the boiling
so it doesn't boil

Solution: We need to keep stirring faster

Be how you were, be how you were

82.

Then cut me so I unfold like the sky between
leaves into a string of paper dolls either
holding hands

83.

I brace still at traces: confetti, floss

These thoughts you put in me

I want you more than things better

84.

Singing: *We can no more*
than can no more
than can no more . . .

85.

In the photograph, you couldn't tell
if the robin was adding a ribbon to its nest or pulling
one from it

86.

Holding out for versus reaching out for

Holding back from versus reaching back from

Holding onto versus reaching onto

87.

I sang: *I held your breasts*
like a single breast

My cheek is softer where it touched
your neck

88.

The dog has worn a circle around its post bare, chain
a clock hand

It is not our dog, we release it

89.

So you asked why one side of the geese
V is longer

Of the geese V we saw lodged in an elm

It has more geese in it

90.

Every breath, a crutch

91.

Dandelions miners' headlamps

92.

I sang: *What is love to a fault?*

93.

You sang: *We drank the sun when it glowed in broth*

It very rarely did, it very rarely did

94.

Then that month in actual Seattle when you said you couldn't
sleep if I was watching so I left

to watch fire-escapes, afraid they might sleep if I didn't

Noticing first the way the pulley release mechanism that separates
the last rung from the sidewalk takes two to land

And how unbearable when that gap is less than a foot, but still

95.

Then second: can the metal melt?

96.

Third: if I were asked to write a guidebook
for young fire-escapes I would need to tell them they are ribs
without hearts unless they are filled
by fire with people who want only

As any good heart would . . .

What runs through you, running you through . . .

Passion rhymed to passing . . .

97.

The knife appears curved because it is near the guitar

I sang: *Their waists such finely broken ankles are*

98.

If any meet my eyes, they'll know

They'll send them back

99.

Even instinct isn't instant

As the unfaded section of wall paint where a painting was
with still the label by it, *Winter*

100.

Snow coming now like tissue after tissue from a box

101.

This window propped by the street I
see through it

I hide myself in brightness

102.

The plane never lands

103.

Then now the sense of perpetuity, who could ever wait
between eating and swimming?

Not eat one cough drop after another?

Not start every letter, despite nothing happening:
This morning, I?

104.

Or not draw a small V as though a gull seen
from a distance or a migration
of geese every time
through the day I think of you every
minute

105.

Then dressed for you, as the avalanche in
a bedsheet, and leapt
from a stepladder at your cue:

I sent the rain to tell you I haven't died

Which I made you repeat because I loved the sound
and suspense of it, as though forgetting the cue

106.

And sang: *Each hummingbird the weight of a testicle*

Send the rain to tell me you haven't died

107.

We don't do much except paint over the stains
or rub them around so

As though you can clean simply
by rubbing

Or heal enough likewise, if you can ever
heal enough, either by work or rest, the other

108.

Outlast this song

109.

You who read with lips moving always only
breathing in, exhaling only
to turn a page

110.

If I say the tea is sweet, does it matter how?

111.

And I sang: *Isn't it also balance, to be always flinging?*

112.

Dawn a sieve, a nerve, a seizing up

113.

And I sang: *Please don't do to me as I have*

And: *I do not wish*

And: *Tell me of the heart that exists*

A Children's Story (On a Theme from Donald Justice)

for Jay Thompson

Much of his life occurred some years ago like little
snow thickening in a lane the white
in her teeth and eyes moved him like childhood

loss, as though they were already
former lovers. March she stood like a church with plains
around it even with Chicago

around it how lazily memory has it all the missing depths and rain
blown in toward our dishes like dust
in turning light as this girl put on one of Mozart's minor

symphonies. Who wouldn't want to think of it
they sped their pace to leave the others she moved like wind near
a church on the plains his body felt a few degrees of change.

Privately

Bent nail sun

I try to see

The mountains farther off

To make the moon

Draw in

*

One issue is understanding doesn't change a thing but one
doesn't want understanding but
the things

A book that does not contain the word *fountain*

Even to scale the mountain again is memory

*

Moon bright enough

To read

By one proves by reading

His hand

*

To change one's conception of the possible you
may change any conception of the impossible

As in, "Impossible for a book to not contain . . ."

*

Applause at

The introduction bleeding

Into an opening

*

If you walk away now I will see you as leaving
always sheets in the morning or if nearing
returning into

*

Fond as a

Sofa on the porch of the first

House we owned

*

The x-rays were interesting only when one knew the exteriors
they were of and could touch
the for example orchid or unusually heavy antique

*

Sunday and other

Sorts of music

The canal

*

In another life, the man and woman of these windows
moving in the canal call wind

in the orchard The Fruit of the Orchard, she smiles

to him as to herself, chorus extending long enough
you lean each time enlivened more slightly toward me
in. Chorus: *Shaken from the tree the fruit*

continues shaking. Moveable type of birds, name, name
name, name, name. In another life, tending
her morning with this tea's steam, and daren't look away

Real Time

In another life, they watch one dance in the square
tide up through cobbles, watching not themselves moving then

a turned bed, apple *fog* from a cart, man offloading
his satchel of styrofoam shavings to water. He returns

waves his hand before him for the string that is the light,
and quieting at her socks on the sill canal stiff on the glass,

one on crutches toppled from a taller bridge *she wakes*
and will not love you less

*

The shared

Imagining of distance

A kind of closeness

Evening settles

*

Reading together is mostly looking up

The world a more literal place this morning

Standing not with a loaf but the flour

Deep Cover

Little houses on a smaller street

Caved-in face

I dream I am touching your fingers for rings

*

To love

To the

Exclusion of—

*

Light so full in the window you can't see out the fountain
above the chopped salad streets of the mountain
town in the valley like an upset skirt

White long from breast to throat bones like names struck
on interdepartmental envelopes

*

A man outside

Twice their ages together

Stands on a picnic table

Watering plums

He gave them at breakfast

*

Dawn dangling

Like a cat toy

You can eat the seeds

*

Immoderate, as all beloved was

I see you looking off, thoughtlessly, reading

A book one could read anywhere

*

Her handwriting alone an aphrodisiac, like crushed fern leaves and the gummy bitten marrow. He felt he could reconstruct her from it. Or at least a room for her, the spiraling stairs, skylight. Mirrors of varied size. Varnished frames, wall of books. Alcove surrounded with indirecting sun. She wrote while drinking coffee, leaning back so it would not touch the page (she always dribbled), days of elaborate breakfast—

Under them later parasols and later vendors and the men breaking the night's bottles to gather them. She waits turns as the fan catching. Kindly casual at last his shirt on the chair, a kind of fighting then forgives through this. Morning crosses its arms, crosses them. One understands this is all that may be, as though we have a choice or wish to understand—

*

Painful in the way memory is, the existing in fact

Marble dusk absorbs

*

You would like this after lunch, asleep

*

Candles set

Off in the floating

River

Cardinal Song

for Molly Marie

You wake and say the sound is cardinal song

A kind of orienting temperance

Toilet paper spiral-iced in trees until trunks turn white

Old gods seen through perfecting distances

Song an ancient priestess heard while setting blade

To the throat of an orange boar (signal of spring)

To stay a hand

Today, I promise, speak of the mail it will still come

All long-awaited correspondences

Will come like soldiers' boats on a cancelled shore

Delible the one
called morning is
a young woman
in a field with a scythe :

the guide we paid   to lead us from the city   returned us to the city

improbable the artist lived thirteen years after the self-portrait

Reversible Sun
like an
extension of
the human
hand the heart
conditions [do you know what birdlime is?] / *leans back as when*

> *saying grace or after*
> *taking up*
> *a hand of cards*

Thin Horse
in its ruins
paddock cants
if the parents die
immediately
it is a children's story;
goats among
the ocher gorse   broken cores
leeching seeds   as burrs germinate
in fur to burst
and bees fat
with apple honey   hum on your polished   abalone

Humility is not
a satisfied virtue [you know what's lye?]
the cardinal knows only
the redness of
its mate : what is *through everything*   without everything? /
b) lace sling   c) crutch of lyre
for my vows, I point:
the ground is right where I left it   you know, the ancients
called this indulgence
Sacrifice
a tree shorn by power lines
tree rent by lightning   she peeled down the bark to see the live wood scar

Mirror Dark
as a diving
bird's back   so predators see only   depth

As a man traveling
to his beloved
might be led to a far pasture
to see a donkey born [will you be the roof or the rain the canvas all
orange or orange-slashed?]

As the first
guidebooks   were etiquettes
on how to see

d) small glass swan in my arm

Of the Emperor's
many questions   noble blood

e) You will need a bigger fire if you are to see me

The angel
had wings
all over,
at street level   the river moves   just enough
to turn bodies in place [calendar I carved days in the tree and the tree
grew back the canoe maker shipwrecked with only the canoe he came in
fashioned a thousand useless miniature canoes from it];

f) had to be cold long time before could be the fire in the snow

The Gallery's
illuminations show us
the damned,   with eyes,   and everything

(leaves   that fell in autumn   rising now)

City

for Melissa Dickey and Andy Stallings

A handkerchief on a stick can hold little but another handkerchief, or an apple, which could itself be held on a stick. Music next door a variety of dumbwaiter. What's that sound she said he said the wind in the train station no she said the other he the people there. *If it would only, if it would just.* Hands on the ground as if peeling or bracing or to resuscitate. Immediate auscultation: an ear to the chest to hear its rattle, shakes you (have seen a man diagnose a dance hall).

*

To know enough of the language to come across as one who is silent. Assent a closed hand, conviction a fist. Said: possession tied to departure (*we have to leave*). Then: my good heart, as though (*my good arm*). I button the dress, I remove a speck from the hair; in the hour before the metro shuts down, you can feel it getting tired. The men and statues and horses in the painting all the same paint. Shadow across the road a detour, as in, the word for having never imagined.

Of course one never touches particularly any part of the body until injury and it feels odd. Can be more public to wander alone and watch things or speak with another in a small room. A path formed along the wall. Or swallowing: sips too small. Subcutaneous, as in, undercuts. However, you look at it (an hour to unwrap a peppermint by tongue).

*

Walking home holding a hand as staring into a darkened garden, 4 rue Fabert. Shows her breasts to the jumper. Bent back to see the tall Thing until staring behind that is the past you saw. The figure an excuse for sky. By the time the symptoms show. Taking months to see one across the square (crossing as a calendar square). As figures on a distant lawn. Siren's note which changes as it passes or it is several sirens.

Searching for the one thing not on the map to learn the map. The way Boulevard St. X which I know comes after a week to bisect Boulevard St. Y which I also know (love). If you do the trick right, a magician appears. A window appears (beneath every window: this is the tomb of). Not walking up walls but the footprints. Singing: *we need to talk.* Answer: roofs, the cinema, streets (named for where they lead). Answer: an egg, the shutters, seeds in a melon. Sighs seeds. So I gather (lust leaves me, leads me).

*

Hello, megaphone. Agreeing with this look to finish the drinks. Every order (ultimately): chronological. To speak a perfect language. Things I wanted to film but couldn't. Staunching with spider webs oil and vinegar. Fisherman so poor he found an infant in clover. Women carry the sheets in a sheet. Thing seen in reverse most startling when then forwarded. It is an apple, or the mouth.

Fruit the color of the sky, apples blue. A hat, an aspect, flight. Eyes represented by small birds at a fountain (if I am a day). As when you dream you're awake and I say what did you say and you wake and say what did I say. The watch changes itself as though nothing has changed. Handprint on the mirror three nights old and between me and the mirror you touching the mirror. "Section reserved for silent prayer." As it happens (the only spot from which one can see the contemporary metropolis). Sebastian swoons through arrows.

*

So prisoners build the maze they tunnel out, cannot be tracked as long as they never surface. He examines the window, and then he examines the skull (gnats). Sleep in the shade of the tree with a jug until the shade is the shape of the jug. The guards in booths like salesmen at telephones waiting out rain (not caring for rain). Scanning the horizon, or shaking the head.

Like always, all at once, sunrise, as a lost child counting higher and higher in woods. As poppy seeds in a cake. Oxen on copper (the downpour). *Quail* for *avail*. *Then* for *than* (as though everything temporized). The old woman next door wakes to say there are people in the street (her son killed himself and her husband the concierge fell from a ladder and died before that). Staying awake as though it will save. Stunned, all right. If you are a tripod, the third leg is your gaze and the camera who knows.

*

Car going faster or posts grown closer together. Men pronouncing the names of fish.

An exhalation, or the word for egg. Mirror turns anything a martyr (I hold the book open and call whatever I do reading). Can always paint your room. As one who can't get right thinks maybe there is no right (or readying myself for a righter). To come to a street behind the street, rougher. Peeled the orange from inside (orange on a welder's pike). Whatever the book is missing from the shelf, let's want. Chestnut trees and newspaper men. "Childhood is full of smells" (Cocteau).

"To what can the arms not be held out?" (Michaux). A wall with two bricks hovering before it (a brick wall). A pond with two fish hovering above it (only two fish in the pond). You at the corner, me at two streets. One in the furrow, one in the field. Knife hid in fruit. Or to reach into any aspect of the hay. Tinned day (boats boathouse color, rain housepaint shade). Bouquets thrown to the stage: the last dancers.

*

The church, and the church in snow; the hills, and their sides. "Study for a Woman Waking." "Nocturne Without Moon." Could go to sleep in the bushes and wake and it will be like a fairy tale only nothing will change. "Path Before the Bride Appears."

Acknowledgments

I'm grateful to the journals that first published this book's poems: *Black Warrior Review, Burnside Review, Court Green, Double Room, Filter, Handsome, Hannah, I Thought I Was New Here, Jellyfish, Omnidawn Blog, Poetry Northwest, Route 9,* and *Verse Online.*

I'd also like to thank the MFA Program for Poets and Writers at the University of Massachusetts Amherst, the Daniel and Merrily Glosband Fellowship, Kenyon College, *Alligator Juniper,* Exploding Swan Operations, sp ce studio, and the Poetry Society of America. Thank you, also, Donald Revell, Cole Swensen, Kazim Ali, Stephanie G'Schwind, and my friends and family.

This book was set in Adobe Jenson Pro,
a typeface designed by Robert Slimbach,
by the Center for Literary Publishing
at Colorado State University.
Cover design by Drew Nolte,
cover photo by Pál Csonka,
book design by Stephanie G'Schwind,
and printing by BookMobile.